THE
WORLD'S WEIRDEST
ANIMALS

CLARE HIBBERT

D0505148

TYNNWYD O STOC
WITHDRAWN

ARCTURUS

ARCTURUS

This edition published in 2011 by Arcturus Publishing Limited
26/27 Bickels Yard, 151–153 Bermondsey Street,
London SE1 3HA

Copyright © 2011 Arcturus Publishing Limited

All rights reserved. No part of this publication may be reproduced, stored in a retrieval
system, or transmitted, in any form or by any means, electronic, mechanical, photocopying,
recording or otherwise, without prior written permission in accordance with the provisions of
the Copyright Act 1956 (as amended). Any person or persons who do any unauthorised act in
relation to this publication may be liable to criminal prosecution and civil claims for damages.

The right of Clare Hibbert to be identified as the author of this work has been asserted by her
in accordance with the Copyright, Designs and Patents Act 1988.

ISBN: 978-1-84858-085-5
CH001960EN
Supplier 05, Date 0911, Print run 1102

Printed in Singapore

Editor for Arcturus Publishing: Joe Harris
Design: sprout.uk.com

Series concept: Discovery Books Ltd, 2 College Street, Ludlow, Shropshire SY8 1AN
www.discoverybooks.net
Managing editor for Discovery Books: Paul Humphrey
Editor and picture researcher for Discovery Books: Clare Hibbert

THE WORLD'S WEIRDEST ANIMALS

CLARE HIBBERT

CONTENTS

THE WORLD'S WEIRDEST

FISH

Get ready to dive into the world of strange sea creatures. In this chapter, we uncover the world's freakiest fish – from spiky pufferfish to glow-in-the-dark monsters of the deep.

There are no prizes for guessing why this is called a blob fish! The blob fish doesn't move much. Instead it sits and waits for its food to drift by.

BLOB FISH FACTS

SIZE: up to 30 cm (12 inches) across
HOME: deep waters off Australia
EATS: any small morsels that float by

Scientists don't know much about the blob fish – except that it's under threat. It's inedible, but trawlers net it while fishing for crabs and lobsters. This one certainly doesn't look very cheerful, does it?

BLOB FISH

WEIRD OR WHAT?

The blob fish's jelly-like flesh is slightly lighter than water. This means the fish can float just above the seabed without using any energy.

Rosy-Lipped Batfish

Look at this glamour puss! The rosy-lipped batfish isn't a good swimmer, but has modified fins that allow it to walk across the seabed. They make it look like it has legs!

WEIRD OR WHAT?

The batfish has a lure of frilly flesh on its forehead that tempts prey close enough to eat.

The fish's red 'lipstick' helps other rosy-lipped batfish recognize it at spawning time.

ROSY-LIPPED BATFISH FACTS

SIZE: up to 36 cm (14 inches) long
HOME: off Cocos Island, Costa Rica
EATS: small fish, crustaceans
(shrimps, molluscs, crabs)

Frogfish

Frogfish live in warm, shallow seas. There are about 60 different species. Some blend in with the seabed and others with their colourful coral-reef surroundings.

WEIRD OR WHAT?

Some frogfish can change colour to match their surroundings.

Like batfish, frogfish have leg-like pectoral fins. They use these to crawl slowly across the seabed.

10

Most frogfish are bottom dwellers. This shaggy looking beast is a hairy frogfish! It feeds on flounders and other flatfish.

FROGFISH FACTS

SIZE: up to 30 cm (12 inches) long
HOME: tropical and subtropical waters worldwide
EATS: crustaceans, fish (including other frogfish)

New frogfish species are still being found. This one, the psychedelic frogfish, was discovered off the coast of Indonesia in 2008. Its pattern matches the stripy corals in which it lives.

STONEFISH

STONEFISH FACTS

SIZE: 35 cm (13 inches) long
HOME: shallow, tropical waters of the Indo-Pacific
EATS: small fish, shrimps

Is it a piece of weed-covered rock, or a fish? Stonefish are disguised to look like stones lying on the seabed. This camouflage hides them from prey and predators, such as bottom-feeding sharks and rays.

Stonefish have another defence, too – a row of needle-like spines on their back that can inject deadly venom.

WEIRD OR WHAT?

Stonefish venom can kill a person within two hours - unless he or she is treated in time with antivenom.

This fish isn't called 'sarcastic' because it makes harsh remarks. Sarcastic originally meant 'tearing of flesh'. Sarcastic fringeheads are certainly very aggressive. They defend their territory from other fringeheads by tussling with their mouths.

SARCASTIC FRINGEHEAD FACTS

SIZE: up to 30 cm (12 inches) long, but usually 15 cm (6 inches)
HOME: off the Pacific coast of the USA
EATS: small crustaceans

SARCASTIC FRINGEHEAD

WEIRD OR WHAT?

If it can't find a rocky crevice, a sarcastic fringehead may set up home in an empty snail shell or even an old bottle!

The fringehead squashes itself into a crevice but pops out to ambush prey. The hidey-hole also protects its scaleless body.

JAWFISH

Jawfish have outsized jaws. Like sarcastic fringeheads, they fight one another in mouth-wrestling competitions.

JAWFISH FACTS

SIZE: up to 10 cm (4 inches) long
HOME: Atlantic, Indian and Pacific oceans
EATS: small invertebrates

The jawfish also tunnels with its mouth. It scoops up a mouthful of sand and transports it elsewhere, gradually hollowing out a home.

WEIRD OR WHAT?

Jawfish are mouth brooders. They look after their eggs inside their mouths until they hatch.

Leafy Sea Dragon

Now you see it; now you don't! The leafy sea dragon is named for the flaps of skin all over its body that look just like seaweed. They provide brilliant camouflage!

WEIRD OR WHAT?

Female sea dragons lay their eggs in a pouch on the male's tail. He looks after them until they hatch.

LEAFY SEA DRAGON FACTS

SIZE: up to 24 cm (10 inches) long

HOME: off the coast of Australia

EATS: shrimps, sea lice, fish fry

Sea dragons are relatives of sea horses. They have a mouth like a drinking straw for sucking up tiny shrimps.

LIONFISH

Lionfish live in coral reefs. They're named for their impressive 'mane' of stripy spines.

LIONFISH FACTS

SIZE: around 30 cm (12 inches) long
HOME: the Pacific Ocean, but they've recently spread to the Caribbean and Mediterranean
EATS: small fish, crustaceans

These spines may look pretty, but they're very dangerous. Each one is coated in venomous mucus. You wouldn't want to step on one of these while swimming!

WEIRD OR WHAT?

Lionfish are pests in parts of the Caribbean. They prey on native fish and have no natural predators. Fishermen who catch them and hand them in are paid a reward!

Lionfish sometimes herd their fish or shrimp prey into a corner before tucking in.

PARROTFISH

Parrotfish change colour at different stages in their development. Most parrotfish start out female and later change into males. Imagine that!

This fish has a beak like a parrot, but it can't talk! Parrotfish use their beaks to scrape algae off rocks and corals.

PARROTFISH FACTS

SIZE: 30-100 cm (12-40 inches) long, depending on species
HOME: tropical and subtropical shallows worldwide
EATS: algae, coral polyps

WEIRD OR WHAT?

Some parrotfish wear pyjamas! At night they wrap up their body in a coating of mucus. Scientists think it makes them more difficult for eels and other hunters to sniff out.

PUFFERFISH

BEFORE

Pufferfish can puff up like a balloon. This defence makes them too much of a mouthful for most predators – especially since many species are covered in prickles. They're poisonous, too!

PUFFERFISH FACTS

SIZE: 2.5-90 cm (1-35 inches) long, depending on species

HOME: usually tropical waters

EATS: algae, invertebrates (e.g. sponges, sea urchins)

AFTER

WEIRD OR WHAT?

In Japan the poisonous flesh of the pufferfish - fugu - is a delicacy. Only trained chefs can prepare it.

Pufferfish rely on sight to find their food. They can move each eye independently.

OCEAN SUNFISH

The ocean sunfish is no beauty, but it is the world's heaviest bony fish. It starts life measuring just a millimetre or so, but eventually weighs about 1,000 kilograms (1 ton).

WEIRD OR WHAT?

Ocean sunfish females produce more eggs than any other vertebrate – as many as 300 million at a time! How would you like that many brothers and sisters?

OCEAN SUNFISH FACTS

SIZE: usually up to 1.5 m (5 feet)
HOME: open ocean, tropical to temperate waters
EATS: jellyfish, fish, crustaceans

The sunfish is named for its habit of 'sunbathing' at the surface. It may do this to encourage seagulls, which land and pick off parasites!

OARFISH

The four species of oarfish are true 'monsters of the deep'. This giant oarfish is the world's longest bony fish. It usually grows to about 9 m (30 feet), but there have been reports of fish as long as 17 m (55 feet).

WEIRD OR WHAT?

Myths about sea serpents might be based on sightings of oarfish.

Oarfish spend most of their time in deep water. They sometimes swim in an upright pose.

OARFISH FACTS

SIZE: usually 9 m (30 feet) long
HOME: deep waters of tropical and subtropical seas
EATS: zooplankton (e.g. tiny crustaceans), jellyfish, squid, small fish

PELICAN EEL

The pelican eel is a deep-sea weirdo. It's named for its elastic mouth, which resembles a pelican bird's stretchy throat.

PELICAN EEL FACTS

SIZE: about 1 m (3 feet) long
HOME: deep waters of tropical and subtropical seas
EATS: small crustaceans

WEIRD OR WHAT?

The pelican eel produces red flashing lights from its tail, probably to attract prey in the gloomy deep where it lives.

The fish's gaping mouth is about 25 cm (10 inches) long. The rest of its body is snake-like.

Most fish soon die if they are taken out of the water — but not the mudskipper. It can breathe on land as well as under water.

MUDSKIPPER FACTS

SIZE: 30 cm (12 inches) long
HOME: tropical swamps and estuaries around the Indo-Pacific
EATS: small crustaceans

WEIRD OR WHAT?

Mudskippers take in oxygen from the air through their skin. They also save bubbles of air in their gills.

MUDSKIPPER

Mudskippers live in coastal regions. When the tide goes out, they walk or skip around the mud flats looking for food.

WEIRD OR WHAT?

Coelacanth eggs develop inside the mother's body, perhaps for as long as three years. Then the mother gives birth to about five well-developed young.

COELACANTH

For a long time scientists only knew about the coelacanth from fossils, like the one above. This fossil is 150 million years old.

COELACANTH FACTS

SIZE: around 1.5 m (5 feet) long
HOME: deep waters of the Indo-Pacific
EATS: fish, squid

Scientists thought that coelacanths had become extinct millions of years ago. But then in 1938 a live coelacanth was caught!

ARCHER FISH

No fish can match the archer fish at target practice!

WEIRD OR WHAT?

The archer fish can hit prey from a distance of 1.5 m (5 feet).

When the fish spots a creepy-crawly on an overhanging plant, it shoots a jet of 'spit' at it. Gotcha! The prey falls into the water and the fish gobbles it up.

ARCHER FISH FACTS

SIZE: 5–40 cm (2–15 inches) long

HOME: fresh and coastal waters around the Indo-Pacific

EATS: insects, spiders

FLYING FISH

Is it a bird or is it a fish?
Flying fish have a neat trick for escaping
marine predators – they leave the water! Swimming
at top speed, the fish can break through the
surface and glide through the air.

FLYING FISH FACTS

SIZE: 45 cm (17 inches) long
HOME: tropical and subtropical
waters worldwide
EATS: plankton

WEIRD OR WHAT?

A flying fish can cover
up to 180 m (590 feet)
in a single glide.

The fish glide on stiff,
outstretched pectoral fins. Their
average gliding speed is about
16 km (10 miles) per hour.

FANGTOOTH

This fish looks like a monster from outer space! Thanks to its long, needle-sharp teeth, the fangtooth is one of the fiercest looking fish in the sea. It lives in the deepest parts of the ocean.

WEIRD OR WHAT?

When it shuts its mouth, the fangtooth houses its longest lower fangs in two special sockets on either side of its brain.

This fangtooth baby, or larva, has protective spines to put off predators.

FANGTOOTH FACTS

SIZE: up to 16 cm (6 inches) long
HOME: deep waters worldwide
EATS: anything that passes by

ANGLERFISH

All anglerfish have a lure that dangles above their face, tempting prey to come near. The deep-sea anglerfish's lure glows in the dark, so it can be seen through the gloom.

lure

WEIRD OR WHAT?

Some male anglerfish live like parasites on the body of a much bigger female. She may carry as many as six males at a time.

ANGLERFISH FACTS

SIZE: females: 18 cm (7 inches), males: 3 cm (1 inch)
HOME: deep waters worldwide
EATS: small fish, crustaceans

THE WORLD'S WEIRDEST

SNAKES AND LIZARDS

Here be dragons! That's right –
real-life ones. In this chapter, we encounter
the world's most remarkable reptiles, from peculiar
pythons to camouflaged chameleons.

This funny fellow must be the Triceratops of the lizard world! It is a male Jackson's chameleon. Most of the time it appears green, but it can also change its skin colour.

CHAMELEON

CHAMELEON FACTS

SIZE: 3-68 cm (1-26 inches) long, depending on species

HOME: Africa, southern Europe, parts of Asia

EATS: insects

Chameleons change colour to blend in with their surroundings – or simply to show their mood or health.

This colourful customer is a panther chameleon. Its curled-up tail is brilliant at gripping – it acts as a fifth limb.

WEIRD OR WHAT?

A chameleon can rotate and focus each eye separately. This gives it excellent all-round vision for pinpointing the position of prey.

Chameleons eat locusts and other insect prey. They shoot their long, sticky tongues out and in again too fast for the human eye to see.

31

BASILISK LIZARD

Basilisk lizards live near rainforest streams, and can race over the surface of the water to escape danger. They can cross a 3 m (10 foot) stream in just two seconds.

These lizards are nicknamed Jesus Christ lizards, after the Bible story in which Jesus walks across the Sea of Galilee.

WEIRD OR WHAT?

Basilisk lizards are good swimmers. They can stay underwater for up to half-an-hour.

Basilisks often have speckles or stripes on their greenish-brown skin. This patterning provides excellent camouflage in their forest home.

Basilisk lizards have
a lightweight, skinny body and a
long, whip-like tail. Some have a sail,
like the dinosaur Spinosaurus, along
their back and tail.

BASILISK LIZARD FACTS

SIZE: up to 1 m (3 feet) long
HOME: rainforests, Central
        and South America
EATS: insects, fruit, flowers,
        fish, snakes, birds,
        eggs, rodents

The basilisk is named after
a mythical monster that was
half-cockerel, half-snake. Its crest
looks a bit like a cock's comb.

FRILLED LIZARD

FRILLED LIZARD FACTS

SIZE: 1 m (3 feet) long
HOME: rainforests, Australasia
EATS: mostly insects, also spiders, lizards, small mammals

'Look how big and scary I am!' this lizard seems to be saying. The frilled lizard has a flap of skin around its neck that makes it look much larger than it really is.

The lizard sticks out the frill by opening its mouth wide. It makes a loud hissing noise at the same time.

If this ferocious display doesn't do the trick, the frilled lizard has a Plan B – it runs away! It races to the nearest tree and climbs high into the branches.

Male frilled lizards use their frill for defence and to scare off rivals. They fight over females at the start of the breeding season.

WEIRD OR WHAT?

Female frilled lizards lay their eggs just under the soil surface. The sex of the babies depends on the weather - in hot conditions, all the babies are female.

ARMADILLO LIZARD

Very few lizards feed their young, but armadillo lizard mums do.

The armadillo lizard has a clever defence. It curls up into a ball, tucking its tail into its mouth. No predator would want to eat that spiky meal!

ARMADILLO LIZARD FACTS

SIZE: 25 cm (10 inches) long
HOME: deserts, Africa
EATS: insects (especially termites), spiders

In the wild, the armadillo lizard lives in dry, desert areas. It's also a popular pet.

36

THORNY DEVIL

Here's another prickly customer! The well-named thorny devil is covered with sharp spines as a defence against predators.

WEIRD OR WHAT?

A thorny devil can eat thousands of ants in a single day.

THORNY DEVIL FACTS

SIZE: 20 cm (8 inches) long
HOME: deserts, Australia
EATS: ants

Komodo dragons are the world's largest lizards.

This lizard may look comical – but as a predator it is no joke. The komodo dragon has a venomous bite which it uses to paralyze prey.

KOMODO DRAGON

Komodo dragons prefer carrion. These dragons are tucking into a dead water buffalo. They eat their meal whole, then cough up the horns, hair and teeth in a pellet.

KOMODO DRAGON FACTS

SIZE: 2-3 m (6-10 feet) long
HOME: Indonesia
EATS: carrion, mammals, invertebrates, reptiles, birds, eggs

This colourful character is a green iguana. Special bacteria in its gut help it to digest plant foods such as buds, flowers, fruit and leaves.

WEIRD OR WHAT?

The marine iguana can dive to depths of 10 m (32 feet).

IGUANA

IGUANA FACTS

SIZE: more than 1.5 m (5 feet) long
HOME: Central and South America
EATS: plants, algae

This marine iguana lives in the Galápagos Islands. It basks on the rocks, but feeds in the sea, nibbling algae off underwater boulders.

Female rock pythons can lay as many as 100 eggs at a time.

AFRICAN ROCK PYTHON

Open wide! Like many snakes, the African rock python can open its lower jaw to swallow prey larger than its own head. This rock python is eating an antelope.

AFRICAN ROCK PYTHON FACTS

SIZE: around 5 m (16 feet) long
HOME: grasslands, sub-Saharan Africa
EATS: rodents, goats, gazelles, warthogs, crocodiles

Pythons kill by constriction – coiling their body tighter and tighter round their prey. The victim suffocates, or dies of a heart attack.

EGG-EATING SNAKE

This nest raider is an egg-eating snake. It climbs trees in search of birds' nests, where it will swallow an egg, shell and all.

WEIRD OR WHAT?

Egg-eating snakes can tell by sniffing whether an egg is fresh or not. They won't eat rotten eggs.

EGG-EATING SNAKE FACTS

SIZE: about 75 cm (30 inches) long
HOME: grasslands, forests, Africa
EATS: birds' eggs

The egg-eating snake doesn't have teeth. Instead spines inside its throat pierce the shell. Then the snake swallows the egg yolk and white and spits out the shell.

This little lizard is a true master of disguise. With its curled-up brown body, the fantastic leaf-tailed gecko looks just like a dead leaf!

Leaf-Tailed Gecko

Fantastic leaf-tailed geckos live on the island of Madagascar. They rely on their cunning camouflage to escape the attention of predators. Can you spot the one in the leaves?

The mossy leaf-tailed gecko goes one better. Like many chameleons, it can change the colour of its skin. This one is blending in with the bark of a tree.

WEIRD OR WHAT?

The spearpoint leaf-tailed gecko is the smallest species. It would fit comfortably in the palm of your hand.

Mossy leaf-tailed geckos also colour themselves to match moss and lichen.

LEAF-TAILED GECKO FACTS

SIZE: 7-30 cm (3-12 inches) long
HOME: forests, Madagascar
EATS: insects, spiders, snails

Tokay Gecko

TOKAY GECKO FACTS

SIZE: about 35 cm (13 inches) long
HOME: rainforests,
      South-East Asia
EATS: insects

All geckos chirp to attract a mate, but the tokay gecko is the noisiest. Its name mimics the sound of its loud, croaky call.

Like many geckos, the tokay gecko has no eyelids. It licks its eyes to stop them drying out in the sun.

WEIRD OR WHAT?

Many tokay geckos now live in cities. Instead of climbing trees for their insect prey, they climb people's walls and ceilings.

Chomp! Chomp! This gila monster is munching a deer mouse.

GILA MONSTER FACTS

SIZE: 60 cm (23 inches) long
HOME: deserts, south-western United States, north-western Mexico
EATS: eggs, chicks, small mammals

GILA MONSTER

The gila monster has a keen sense of smell for tracking down prey. Like all lizards and snakes, it flicks its tongue to detect chemicals in the air.

WEIRD OR WHAT?

This monster has a venomous bite. Rather than being injected, the venom oozes out of grooves on some of the lizard's bottom teeth.

BLUE-TONGUED SKINK

WEIRD OR WHAT?

Like many lizards, skinks can shed their tails, leaving them wiggling to distract a predator while the skink makes a quick getaway.

Doesn't this lizard know it's rude to stick out your tongue?! The blue-tongued skink does this to surprise and ward off predators.

BLUE-TONGUED SKINK FACTS

SIZE: up to 60 cm (23 inches) long
HOME: various habitats, Australia
EATS: insects, spiders, fruit, slugs, snails

The skink's tail confuses eagles and other birds of prey swooping from above. The stumpy shape makes it hard to distinguish the lizard's tail from its head.

SPITTING COBRA

The spitting cobra defends itself from bigger hunters by 'spitting'. It squirts a jet of venom from its fangs directly at an attacker's eyes. The venom can cause blindness.

WEIRD OR WHAT?

A spitting cobra can 'spit' its venom as far as 2 m (6 feet).

Despite their brilliant defence, spitting cobras are still preyed upon. Their main enemies are secretary birds and banded mongooses.

SPITTING COBRA FACTS

SIZE: 120-220 cm (4-7 feet) long
HOME: sub-Saharan Africa
EATS: small mammals, frogs, lizards, snakes

THE WORLD'S WEIRDEST BEETLES

Do creepy crawlies creep you out?
In this chapter, we meet the world's
most bizarre beetles, from bugs that can spray
boiling hot poison to disgusting dung-eaters.

FLOWER BEETLE

FLOWER BEETLE FACTS

SIZE: 0.5-11 cm (0.1-4 inches) long
HOME: worldwide, except Antarctica
EATS: nectar, pollen, fruit

Check out this beetle's funny horn! This is a striped love beetle, but maybe 'y-fronts beetle' would be a better name for it! It uses its horn to fight over females.

Flower beetles use their back wings for flying. Like all beetles, they have hardened front wings that act as protective wing cases.

WEIRD OR WHAT?

Male goliath beetles weigh about the same as a hamster!

Flower beetles include the giants of the insect world. The African goliath beetle can grow longer than 10 cm (4 inches) and it has bigger wings than a sparrow!

Tortoise beetles are a kind of leaf beetle. They feed on leaves and do damage to garden plants. This golden tortoise beetle likes morning glory leaves best.

WEIRD OR WHAT?

The golden tortoise beetle can change colour! Its body can look golden or red, like a ladybird's.

Tortoise Beetle

The tortoise beetle is named for the distinctive shape of its wing cases, which look like a tortoise's shell.

Female tortoise beetles make good mums. This one is looking after her eggs.

TORTOISE BEETLE FACTS

SIZE: up to 1.2 cm (0.5 inches)
HOME: worldwide, especially tropical areas
EATS: leaves

Tortoise beetle larvae stay close to their brothers and sisters. Their bodies are usually spiky to put off birds and other predators.

TIGER BEETLE

The tiger beetle isn't striped, but like its big cat namesake it's a fierce and skilful predator. It runs down prey on its long legs.

WEIRD OR WHAT?

A tiger beetle can speed along at 9 km (5 miles) per hour. Relative to its size, it's more than 20 times faster than an Olympic sprinter!

TIGER BEETLE FACTS

SIZE: up to 2 cm (½ inch) long
HOME: worldwide, especially tropical and subtropical areas
EATS: insects (e.g. ants), other minibeasts (spiders, worms), tadpoles

The tiger beetle uses its long jaws to seize prey and tear it into pieces. Then it spits out saliva to digest the prey before sucking it up.

Some tiger beetles live in trees, but most are ground dwellers. This tiger beetle is hunting among the leaf litter.

Imagine feeding your babies on dung! That's what dung beetles do.

DUNG BEETLE FACTS

SIZE: up to 2.5 cm (1 inch) long
HOME: worldwide, except Antarctica
EATS: dung

DUNG BEETLE

Dung beetles collect animal dung and roll balls of it along the ground. The balls are bigger than the beetles.

WEIRD OR WHAT?

Anyone for tennis? The largest dung balls are as big as tennis balls.

Dung beetles lay their eggs in the dung balls. Their larvae feast on the dung when they hatch.

These duelling minibeasts are stag beetles. The males do battle to win or defend territory.

STAG BEETLE FACTS

SIZE: 1-10 cm (½-4 inches) long
HOME: woodlands, worldwide
EATS: tree sap, rotting fruit
(larvae eat wood)

STAG BEETLE

Stag beetles fight each other with their super-large jaws, or mandibles. These look a bit like stags' antlers, which is how the beetles get their name.

WEIRD OR WHAT?

In some stag beetle species, the jaws make up half of the body length.

There are no prizes for guessing how the rhinoceros beetle got its name!

RHINOCEROS BEETLE

WEIRD OR WHAT?

You could get a surprise if you disturb a rhino beetle. It hisses!

Rhinoceros beetles are a kind of stag beetle. The male has an impressive horn for digging and fighting. It uses its horn to push and shove its rival.

The hercules beetle is one of the largest rhino beetles. Its horn can be 10 cm (4 inches) long.

The hercules beetle is named after the strong hero in ancient Roman myth. It can carry 850 times its own body weight on its shell.

RHINOCEROS BEETLE FACTS

SIZE: 3-13 cm (1-5 inches), excluding horn

HOME: temperate and tropical forests

EATS: nectar, sap, fruit (larvae eat wood)

Do you look like your mum and dad? Beetle babies don't. This is a hercules beetle larva. It spends a couple of years like this, then makes a pupa and changes into its adult form.

WEEVIL

This beetle looks like it has an elephant's trunk! It's an acorn weevil, and uses its long snout to bore into acorns.

All weevils have super-long noses. Most are fussy eaters that feed on just one kind of plant. Some are pests. This red palm weevil damages date and coconut crops.

WEEVIL FACTS

SIZE: up to 6 mm (0.1 inch) long
HOME: worldwide, except Antarctica
EATS: plants

Some weevils are real showstoppers. This one lives in the rainforests of Papua New Guinea.

Most weevils have plain colouring, so that predators don't notice them. These two must win the prize for the best camouflage!

WEIRD OR WHAT?

In North America, boll weevils are a cotton farmer's worst nightmare. Each year they chomp their way through nearly five million bales of cotton.

With its amazingly long neck, this weevil from Madagascar has to be the strangest of all. Its name? The giraffe weevil!

61

Firefly

Check out this glowing bottom! Despite its name, the firefly is a beetle, not a fly.

Fireflies have a neat trick – bioluminescence. This is the ability to make light with their bodies. Fireflies flash to let other fireflies know where they are.

FIREFLY FACTS

SIZE: up to 2.5 cm (1 inch) long
HOME: tropical and temperate areas
EATS: other larvae, snails, slugs, pollen, nectar

WEIRD OR WHAT?

One female firefly uses light as a trap. She mimics the flashes of a different firefly species. When males approach to mate with her, she gobbles them up!

Violin Beetle

With its wide wing cases and long, slim head, this beetle is shaped a bit like a violin.

The beetle's flat body allows it to live under tree bark or among bracket fungi. It uses its slender head to nose about for grubs.

WEIRD OR WHAT?

Don't fiddle with a violin beetle. If threatened, it sprays a chemical powerful enough to paralyze your fingers for 24 hours!

VIOLIN BEETLE FACTS

SIZE: 10 cm (4 inches) long
HOME: rainforests, Malaysia
EATS: insect larvae

BOMBARDIER BEETLE

WEIRD OR WHAT?

Some bombardier beetles can spray as far as a couple of metres!

'Fire!' This bombardier beetle is spraying boiling-hot, poisonous liquid. It does this in self-defence.

BOMBARDIER BEETLE FACTS

SIZE: 2 mm-3 cm (0.1-1 inch) long
HOME: North America, Africa, Asia
EATS: other insects

When the hot fluid comes into contact with the air, it explodes with a loud 'pop!'. The sound, combined with the spray, will see off most predators.

BLISTER BEETLE

WEIRD OR WHAT?

Sometimes blister beetles get into horses' hay. If a horse eats enough of the beetles, it dies.

Ouch! Blister beetles produce a nasty chemical that makes your skin blister.

Bees should tell this blister beetle to 'Buzz off!' Its larvae trick bees into carrying them back to their nest – where they feast on bee eggs!

BLISTER BEETLE FACTS

SIZE: up to 2 cm (½ inch) long
HOME: worldwide, except Antarctica
EATS: insects, flowers, leaves

DIVING BEETLE FACTS

SIZE: 3 cm (1 inch) long
HOME: fresh water
EATS: aquatic insects,
          crustaceans, tadpoles

DIVING BEETLE

This beetle pair are underwater! They are diving beetles, and they live in freshwater streams, rivers and lakes.

Like their parents, diving beetle larvae are fierce predators. They hunt and eat tadpoles and other aquatic prey.

WEIRD OR WHAT?

Great diving beetle larvae are twice as long as their parents!

66

WHIRLIGIG BEETLE

If you look on the surface of a freshwater pond, you may see small groups of little shiny beetles.

WEIRD OR WHAT?

Whirligig beetles have two-part eyes, so they can see above and below the surface of the water at the same time.

Whirligig beetles are named for their behaviour when they are threatened – they whirl round and round in circles.

Like shoaling fish, whirligig beetles hang out in a group to avoid being eaten.

WHIRLIGIG BEETLE FACTS

SIZE: up to 3.5 cm (1 inch) long
HOME: fresh water
EATS: aquatic insects

THE WORLD'S WEIRDEST
BIRDS

Watch the birdie! In this chapter, we
discover the wackiest winged wonders
of the bird kingdom, from speedy roadrunners
to stretchy-throated pelicans.

COCK OF THE ROCK

With their crazy crests, cocks of the rock are the punks of the bird world! They're one of the brightest coloured birds in the South American rainforest.

WEIRD OR WHAT?

Cocks of the rock are named for their habit of nesting in holes on cliff faces.

COCK OF THE ROCK FACTS

SIZE: 32 cm (12 inches) long
HOME: tropical and subtropical rainforests, South America
EATS: fruit, insects, small reptiles

Bright colours attract the notice of predators as well as mates. Eagles, hawks, jaguars and boa constrictors all hunt cocks of the rock.

KING VULTURE

Like many vultures, the king vulture is a scavenger. Having a bald neck and head helps it to avoid getting blood all over its feathers when feasting on carrion.

WEIRD OR WHAT?

King vultures can only croak and wheeze, as they don't have a voice box.

The king vulture is far more colourful than most vultures. The skin on its neck can be orange, red, yellow or purple.

KING VULTURE FACTS

SIZE: up to 80 cm (30 inches) long
HOME: tropical forests, Central and South America
EATS: carrion

HORNBILL

Hornbills are named for their long, horny beaks. Most of them, including this rhinoceros hornbill, have an odd, helmet-like structure on their bill. Imagine carrying that around on your head all the time!

HORNBILL FACTS

SIZE: 40-160 cm (15-62 inches) long
HOME: tropical and subtropical Africa and Asia
EATS: fruit, insects, small animals

Hornbills mostly eat fruit. This hornbill is about to gobble down a chunk of juicy papaya.

Hornbill dads imprison their families in their nests! The male seals in the female and her eggs to keep them safe from predators. He leaves a small hole to pass food through to his family.

This is a wrinkled hornbill. The beak is not wrinkly because of old age. The grooves on it were there from the moment it hatched.

WEIRD OR WHAT?

Male hornbills sometimes use their beaks to bash rivals – in mid-air!

BIRD of PARADISE

The bird of paradise family includes some of the bird world's biggest show-offs. In many species, like this greater bird of paradise, the males have trailing ornamental feathers, called plumes.

WEIRD OR WHAT?

The loudest bird of paradise is the well-named trumpet bird.

BIRD OF PARADISE FACTS

SIZE: 15-45 cm (6-18 inches) long
HOME: tropical forests of Australasia, southern Asia, South America
EATS: fruit, spiders

This raggiana bird of paradise male is displaying to attract a mate. He fans out his feathers and prances and bobs. It's lucky the females have a good attention span because these dances can go on for hours!

Wilson's bird of paradise lives in the rainforests of Indonesia. The male's tail plumes form two tight curls. Its body is black with bright splashes of blue, red and yellow.

Fancy colours are important in the gloomy shade of the rainforest because they catch a female's eye. She knows by looking at his glossy feathers that a male is healthy, and that he'll make a good dad for her chicks.

This has to win the 'best nest' award! It's the work of a male bowerbird. He builds a shelter, or bower, out of twigs and grasses.

BOWERBIRD FACTS

SIZE: up to 40 cm (15 inches) long
HOME: forests and scrubland, Australasia
EATS: fruit, flowers, insects

BOWERBIRD

WEIRD OR WHAT?

Some bowerbirds 'paint' their bowers. They make the paint from chewed-up leaves and spit.

The bowerbird puts together an eye-catching display to impress his mate. He arranges piles of colourful objects, including shells, fruit, feathers and even clothes pegs!

SHOEBILL

The shoebill is a kind of stork. It gets its name from the clog-like shape of its wide, thick bill.

WEIRD OR WHAT?

The shoebill's favourite food is lungfish – air-breathing fish that live among the plants on the banks of the River Nile.

Shoebills are large birds with big appetites. They cruise over rivers and marshes looking for slippery fish, turtles and even baby crocodiles!

SHOEBILL FACTS

SIZE: 1.2 m (3½ feet) tall
HOME: wetlands, north-eastern Africa
EATS: fish, reptiles

FRIGATE BIRD

Is that red balloon? No – it's the male frigate bird's red throat. This seabird puffs out his throat pouch to attract a mate. The throat can inflate to the size of a human head!

Frigate birds are amazing fliers. They can stay on the wing for a week at a time.

FRIGATE BIRD FACTS

SIZE: 1 m (3 feet) long, with a wingspan of 2 m (7 feet)
HOME: tropical and subtropical coastal waters
EATS: fish

Frigate birds usually have one chick. It doesn't look much like its parents when it hatches, though!

BLUE-FOOTED BOOBY

These birds' feet look like they've been dipped in blue paint!

WEIRD OR WHAT?

'Booby' means a stupid person. Early seafarers called these fearless birds boobies because they were very easy to kill.

Blue-footed boobies are masters of fancy footwork. A courting couple performs a funny, jerky dance, moving their feet up and down and sometimes pointing their beaks at the sky.

BLUE-FOOTED BOOBY FACTS

SIZE: 80 cm (30 inches) long
HOME: Pacific Ocean, from California to the Galápagos Islands
EATS: fish, squid

Weaver Bird

Weaver birds are the champion architects of the bird world. They collect grasses or reeds in their beaks, then use them to weave amazingly intricate nests.

This bright yellow fellow is a cape weaver. See how his nest takes shape. The entrance is at the bottom, to keep it hidden from airborne predators.

1

2

3

WEAVER BIRD FACTS

SIZE: about 20 cm (8 inches) long
HOME: sub-Saharan Africa, parts of Asia and Australia
EATS: seeds, grain, insects

Weavers hang their nest from a branch or support it between a pair of reeds. They like the company of other weavers, so they often nest near neighbours.

Some trees hold 50 or more individual nests. These colonies are extremely noisy.

WEIRD OR WHAT?

Some sociable weaver nests are more than 3 m (10 feet) tall.

Sociable weavers go one better and build a huge nest to share. It is like a block of flats, with individual apartments inside. The biggest nests house more than 100 pairs of weavers.

Look at him go! The roadrunner can run at speeds of 32 km (20 miles) per hour – that's about twice as fast as you on your bike.

ROADRUNNER

WEIRD OR WHAT?

The roadrunner builds its nest in a cactus or small tree. Construction materials include twigs, old snake skins and animal dung. Nice!

Roadrunners will eat pretty much anything – fruit, seeds, creepy crawlies, small reptiles and mammals. This one's snaffled a lizard!

ROADRUNNER FACTS

SIZE: 56 cm (22 inches) long
HOME: deserts of south-western North America
EATS: almost anything!

Kakapo

A parrot that can't fly? Surely not! The kakapo is an extremely rare parrot that lives in New Zealand. It hunts at night, relying on its sense of smell to find prey. Whiskers on either side of its beak help it to feel its way.

WEIRD OR WHAT?

The kakapo lost its ability to fly millions of years ago – probably because there weren't any large land predators in its island home.

KAKAPO FACTS

SIZE: 64 cm (25 in) long
HOME: New Zealand
EATS: leaves, seeds, fruit

PELICAN

Pelicans' beaks are like nature's fishing nets. These birds have super-stretchy throat pouches, which they use to scoop fish out of the water.

PELICAN FACTS

SIZE: 1–1.9 m (3½–6 feet) long
HOME: warm, watery regions worldwide
EATS: fish

WEIRD OR WHAT?

A pelican's pouch can hold more than 10 kg (22 lbs) of fish – three times more fish than the bird has space for in its stomach!

There are about eight species of pelican. These white pelicans live in North America. Like all pelicans, they fly well, but are also strong swimmers.

The secretary bird is named for its distinctive black crest feathers. These feathers look like the quill pens that secretaries used long ago and tucked behind their ears.

Secretary Bird

Thanks to its long legs, the secretary bird is a speedy hunter. It kills its favourite food – snakes – by stamping them to death!

WEIRD OR WHAT?

The secretary bird's scaly legs protect it against snake bites.

SECRETARY BIRD FACTS

SIZE: 1.3 m (4 feet) tall, with a wingspan of 2 m (6½ feet)
HOME: African savannah
EATS: snakes, lizards, grasshoppers, mice, birds' eggs

POTOO

'Aaaghhh!'
This is the strangled cry coming out of the potoo's gaping mouth. Potoos make funny barking noises, too.

WEIRD OR WHAT?

The potoo has slits in its eyelids – so it can see with its eyes shut!

The potoo's brown, mottled feathers disguise it to look like part of a tree. This camouflage hides it by day when it's resting. At night it hunts beetles, moths and other insects.

POTOO FACTS

SIZE: 35 cm (13 inches) long
HOME: tropical and subtropical forests of South America
EATS: insects

TAWNY FROGMOUTH

How many birds can you see? With such excellent camouflage, it's hard to spot the two chicks that this proud parent is guarding!

WEIRD OR WHAT?

The frogmouth gets its name from its wide mouth, not because it eats frogs (although it might make a snack of one very occasionally!).

FROGMOUTH FACTS

SIZE: up to 50 cm (20 inches) long
HOME: southern Asia and Australasia
EATS: insects, small lizards, mice, berries

Like its cousin, the potoo, the tawny frogmouth relies on its colouring to blend in with a branch. If it feels threatened it freezes – being motionless completes the disguise.

THE WORLD'S WEIRDEST BUTTERFLIES AND MOTHS

These creepy creatures will make you go bug-eyed! In this chapter, we investigate the insect world's freakiest flutterers, from see-through butterflies to spooky ghost moths.

CECROPIA MOTH

This moth looks like it's wearing a feather headdress! The cecropia moth is North America's largest moth, and those 'feathers' are its bushy antennae, or feelers.

Like all moths, the cecropia moth uses its antennae to sniff out food and mates.

Moths and butterflies start life as larvae (caterpillars). Caterpillars moult as they grow, losing their outer skin.

A newly-hatched cecropia moth caterpillar is small, black and hairy. After a couple of moults, its body is green with orange and blue knobbly bits!

WEIRD OR WHAT?

Squirrels are bad news for cecropia moths. They snack on their pupae.

The cecropia moth caterpillar goes through four moults, then becomes a pupa. While it is a pupa, it changes into its adult form.

CECROPIA MOTH FACTS

SIZE: wingspan about 13 cm (5 inches)
HOME: North America
EATS: leaves, e.g. maple, cherry and birch (larvae)

GLASSWING BUTTERFLY

GLASSWING BUTTERFLY FACTS

SIZE: wingspan 6 cm (2 inches)
HOME: Central and South America
EATS: cestrum leaves (larvae); nectar (adults)

Most butterfly wings are covered with coloured scales. Some parts of the glasswing's wings do not have these, so they appear see-through.

The glasswing butterfly has see-through windows on its wings!

WEIRD OR WHAT?

Glasswing caterpillars feed on cestrum plants, taking in toxins from the leaves. This makes them poisonous to predators.

Plume moth

The plume moth wins the prize for the weirdest wings! They have long, thin supports with feathery 'plumes' trailing off. They make it look like a spooky ghost moth!

WEIRD OR WHAT?

Plume moths roll up their wings when they are resting.

PLUME MOTH FACTS

SIZE: wingspan of about 3 cm (1 inch)
HOME: grasslands, gardens, worldwide
EATS: leaves and shoots (larvae); nectar (adults)

All moths have leg spurs, but these are especially noticeable in plume moths. The moth uses the spurs to groom its antennae.

PUSS MOTH

WEIRD OR WHAT?

The puss moth caterpillar's head has an extra defensive feature - it can squirt out formic acid.

Just like its namesake, the cat, an adult puss moth has a furry body.

This caterpillar has a ring around its head with two false eyes. These features make the puss moth caterpillar look like a much bigger animal, and confuse predators.

PUSS MOTH FACTS

SIZE: wingspan about 6 cm (2 inches)
HOME: woodlands, Europe, North Africa
EATS: willow and aspen leaves (larvae); nectar (adults)

Owl Butterfly

WEIRD OR WHAT?

'Twit-twoo!' The owl butterfly is named for the huge eyespots on its wings, which look like owls' eyes.

Male owl butterflies hold flying competitions. The females mate with the most talented fliers.

OWL BUTTERFLY FACTS

SIZE: wingspan 14 cm (5½ inches)
HOME: tropical rainforests, Central and South America
EATS: leaves (larvae); juice of rotting fruit (adults)

Most butterflies are active in the day, but the owl butterfly feeds at dusk, when there are fewer birds around that might eat it.

PALE TUSSOCK MOTH

Is this a caterpillar or a feather duster? With its tufty-haired body, the pale tussock moth caterpillar is hard to beat for all-out weirdness.

WEIRD OR WHAT?

Don't get too close to this caterpillar. Brushing against its poison-tipped hairs can give you a nasty rash.

PALE TUSSOCK MOTH FACTS

SIZE: wingspan around 5 cm (2 inches)
HOME: woodlands, Europe
EATS: leaves, e.g. oak, birch, lime and hop (larvae)

The adult moth is far less fancy. Its colouring and markings blend in with its surroundings.

LUNA MOTH

'Luna' means moon. Luna moths are more active at night than during the day.

WEIRD OR WHAT?

A female luna moth lays up to 300 eggs. She lays just five on each leaf, so the caterpillars will have enough food.

LUNA MOTH FACTS

SIZE: wingspan 11 cm (4 inches)
HOME: North America
EATS: leaves, e.g. alder, birch and hickory (larvae)

The adult stage of the luna moth's life lasts about a week. The male relies on its sensitive antennae to locate a female to mate with.

Tent Moth

SIZE: wingspan 2.5 cm (1 inch)
HOME: mostly North America
EATS: leaves (larvae)

This silken structure is a nest built by tent moth caterpillars. They rest when they are not feeding. These monstrous munchers are pests that can strip whole forests.

WEIRD OR WHAT?

A female tent moth may fly hundreds of kilometres to lay her eggs, looking for somewhere with enough food to feed her hungry caterpillars.

DEATH'S-HEAD HAWK MOTH

This moth's spooky name comes from the markings on its body. It looks like a human skull!

WEIRD OR WHAT?

Death's-head hawk moths can mimic the scent of bees. They do this to raid beehives for honey without the bees noticing.

DEATH'S-HEAD HAWK MOTH FACTS

SIZE: wingspan 12 cm (4½ inches)
HOME: Europe, North Africa, Asia
EATS: leaves (larvae); honey (adults)

This is a death's-head hawk moth caterpillar. If disturbed, it makes a clicking noise.

HUMMINGBIRD HAWK MOTH

The hummingbird hawk moth is famous for its super-fast wing beat. The rapid movement makes the wings 'hum' – just like a hummingbird's.

This moth feeds like a hummingbird, too. It uses its long mouthpart to reach deep inside flowers for nectar.

HUMMINGBIRD HAWK MOTH FACTS

SIZE: wingspan up to 4.5 cm (1½ inches)
HOME: Europe, North Africa, Asia
EATS: leaves (larvae); nectar (adults)

WEIRD OR WHAT?

Hummingbird hawk moths return to the same flowerbeds at the same time each day.

Giddy-up! This caterpillar looks like it is wearing a horse's saddle! No wonder it is called the saddleback moth.

SADDLEBACK MOTH

WEIRD OR WHAT?

The saddleback caterpillar has a pair of fleshy horns at either end of its body. These confuse predators, as they do not know which end to attack.

Watch out for the saddleback's hairs. They can give you a nasty sting that leaves a rash on your skin for days.

SADDLEBACK MOTH FACTS

SIZE: wingspan 3.5 cm (1 inch)
HOME: North America
EATS: leaves from woody shrubs (larvae)

Regal Moth

'Regal' means kingly – and with its grand, showy colours, this large moth certainly looks rather royal.

REGAL MOTH FACTS

SIZE: wingspan 15 cm (6 inches)
HOME: woodlands, North America
EATS: leaves of nut trees (larvae)

WEIRD OR WHAT?

Regal moths pupate (turn into a pupa) in an underground burrow, rather than a cocoon.

Its caterpillars are nicknamed hickory horned devils. Among their favourite foods are leaves from hickory trees.

When its wings are closed, the orange oak leaf butterfly looks just like a dead leaf. What brilliant camouflage!

WEIRD OR WHAT?

Orange oak leafs that come out of their pupal stage during the rainy season have stronger colouring than dry-season butterflies.

ORANGE OAK LEAF BUTTERFLY

ORANGE OAK LEAF BUTTERFLY FACTS

SIZE: wingspan 7.5 cm (3 inches)
HOME: tropics, Asia
EATS: leaves (larvae);
nectar (adults)

The butterfly is easier to see with its wings open.

Silk Moth

Silk for clothes comes from the silk moth. Most moth caterpillar species produce silk for their cocoons, but the silk moth's threads are so super-fine that people harvest them to make silk cloth.

The silk moth caterpillar, or silkworm, feeds on mulberry leaves. By the time it is six weeks old, it is more than 7 cm (2½ inches) long.

To spin its cocoon, the silkworm pushes out one strand of silk from its spinneret. This single thread may be nearly 1 km (½ mile) long.

The Chinese have been farming silkworms for nearly 5,000 years. They kept how to do it a closely-guarded secret!

In the wild, the cocoon would have been a safe place to pupate. These days, the only silkworms are farmed ones. The farmer kills the pupae with hot steam, then collects the silken cocoons.

The farmer does allow some of the silk moths to pupate. They will produce the next generation of silkworms.

SILK MOTH FACTS

SIZE: wingspan 5 cm (2 inches)
HOME: native to China, now raised worldwide
EATS: mulberry leaves (larvae)

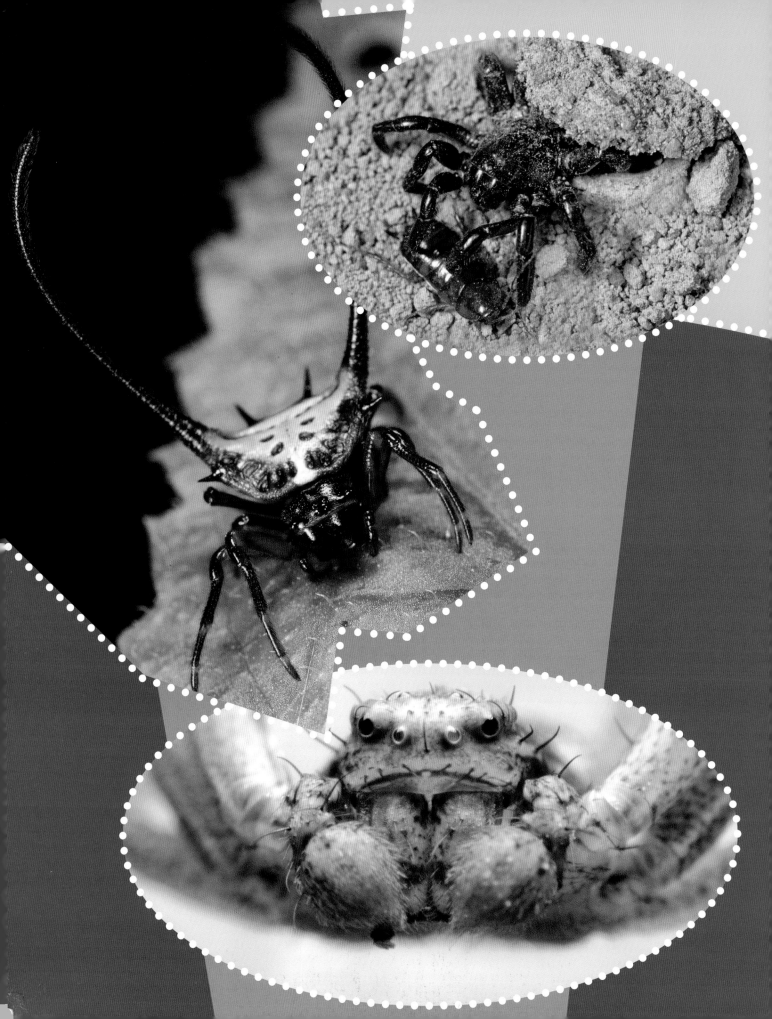

THE WORLD'S WEIRDEST SPIDERS

Let's step into the world of spiders – but don't get caught in their web! In this chapter, meet the most amazing arachnids on earth, from huge bird-eating tarantulas to cunningly camouflaged crab spiders.

ASSASSIN SPIDER

The assassin spider's jaws are a lethal weapon. They are super-long, so the spider can hold its struggling victim away from its body, while it injects venom with its fangs.

ASSASSIN SPIDER FACTS

SIZE: body 2 mm (0.1 inch) long
HOME: forests in Australia, South Africa and Madagascar
EATS: other arachnids

jaws

neck

WEIRD OR WHAT?

The assassin spider has evolved an amazingly long neck. Maybe 'giraffe spider' would be a better name for it!

Everyone knows that spitting is a disgusting habit. But for the slow-moving spitting spider, it's the best way to get a meal.

SPITTING SPIDER

WEIRD OR WHAT?

The spider can target its prey from a distance of more than 1 cm (¼ inch) – that may not sound much, but it's about twice its own body length!

The spider spits a blob of glue and venom at its victim. The glue sticks the prey to the spot and the venom paralyzes it. This spider has just immobilized a mosquito and is moving in for the kill.

SPITTING SPIDER FACTS

SIZE: body 6 mm (½ inch) long
HOME: worldwide
EATS: insects (e.g. mosquitoes, house flies)

BOLAS SPIDER

BOLAS SPIDER FACTS

SIZE: female: body 15 mm (½ inch) long; male: body 2 mm (0.1 inch) long

HOME: America, Africa and Australasia

EATS: moths

Bolas spiders are the gauchos of the arachnid world. Instead of making a web, the spider spins a silken 'bola', a thread with a sticky blob at the end. It swings this towards its prey and… wham! Time for lunch!

This bolas spider, called a magnificent spider, lives in Australia. It is dangling its lasso to rope a passing moth.

There are more than 60 species of bolas spider. Most are picky eaters who feed on one particular moth species.

WEIRD OR WHAT?

A bolas spider has an amazing trick for luring the right kind of male moth victim. It produces pheromones - the special scent female moths give off to attract a mate!

On average, a female bolas spider catches a couple of moths a night. By day she rests – and depends on camouflage to protect her from predators.

SPINY ORB WEAVER

The spiny orb weaver wins the prize for being the punkiest spider! Its body is circled by spikes. Some spiders have six spikes; others as many as ten!

SPINY ORB WEAVER FACTS

SIZE: body 3 cm (1 inch) long
HOME: temperate and tropical forests
EATS: whiteflies, flies, moths, beetles

The spikes – and the bright colours – help to put off forest birds that might be tempted to snack on the spider.

This unusual looking spiny orb weaver has a pair of long horns. It lives in the Malaysian rainforest.

The spider decorates its web with little tufty bits of silk. No one is sure why – maybe it's to make the web more visible to birds that might crash into it.

WEIRD OR WHAT?

Male spiny orb weavers don't have spikes. They have four or five little humps on their back instead.

GOLIATH BIRD-EATING SPIDER

The goliath bird-eater is the world's biggest, scariest, hairiest spider! The size of a dinner plate, it's a kind of tarantula that lives in the Amazon rainforest.

WEIRD OR WHAT?

When threatened, a goliath bird-eater rubs its hairy legs together to produce a loud hissing noise. The sound can be heard 5 m (16 feet) away!

Yikes! This bird-eater has raised its front legs and is about to strike.

BIRD-EATING SPIDER FACTS

SIZE: 30-cm (12-inch) leg span

HOME: South American rainforest

EATS: invertebrates, small reptiles, birds and mammals

This spider has dragged a chick from its nest. The goliath bird-eater has also been known to eat rats, bats, lizards and snakes. More usually, though, it makes a meal of insects and other invertebrates.

Check out these fangs! They can be nearly 4 cm (1½ inches) long. They are used to inject paralyzing venom into prey.

NET-CASTING SPIDER

Forget hanging around on a web hoping for prey! The net-casting spider uses its spinning skills to weave a rectangular net. Then it lies in wait, holding the net in its four front legs.

NET-CASTING SPIDER FACTS

SIZE: body (female) about 2 cm (½ inch) long
HOME: tropical areas worldwide
EATS: insects

When an insect walks by, the spider traps it in the stretchy net. It can catch flying insects too, by flicking the net into the air.

WEIRD OR WHAT?

The net-casting spider is sometimes nicknamed the ogre-faced spider because of its pair of scary, outsized eyes!

The net's not sticky, but it's made from such a tangle of threads that it's almost impossible to escape from.

The net-casting spider is a night hunter. Two of its eight eyes are much bigger than the rest and these give it excellent night vision.

FISHING SPIDER

Fishing spiders have a crafty way of catching food. They lurk on the bank of a pond or stream, resting a foot or two on the water.

When a fishing spider senses ripples, it races across the surface of the water to catch the passing insect or fish.

FISHING SPIDER FACTS

SIZE: the largest females have a leg span of 8 cm (3 inches)

HOME: near fresh water, almost worldwide

EATS: aquatic insects (e.g. mayflies, pond skaters), fish, frogs

Claws at the ends of the fishing spider's front legs help it to keep a firm grip on fast-moving prey. Two of its favourite foods are mayflies and pond skaters.

WEIRD OR WHAT?

Don't laugh at the fishing spider's hairy legs. They repel water, so the spider's body doesn't get wet.

This spider must have fancied a change. It's caught a reed frog to eat.

119

DIVING-BELL SPIDER

Diving-bell spiders spend their lives underwater. They spin themselves a bell-shaped home and fill it with air – just like a mini submarine!

DIVING-BELL SPIDER FACTS

SIZE: body 1 cm (½ inch) long
HOME: freshwater ponds in Europe, northern Asia and north Africa
EATS: aquatic insect larvae, water fleas, *Cyclops* (tiny crustaceans)

WEIRD OR WHAT?

The male diving-bell spider spins a tunnel linking his own diving bell to his mate's!

When air in the bell starts to run out, the spider lets the bell bob back to the surface to collect more bubbles.

The dewdrop spider gets its name from its silvery markings, which make its body look like a shining drop of dew.

DEWDROP SPIDER

DEWDROP SPIDER FACTS

SIZE: body 4 mm–1cm (0.1–½ inch) long
(species vary in length)
HOME: tropics
EATS: tiny insects

This cheeky spider doesn't bother to spin its own web. Instead, it sets up home on a bigger spider's web, and steals its prey.

WEIRD OR WHAT?

Having a dewdrop spider as a squatter isn't necessarily a nuisance. The spider helps its host by clearing away small prey and keeping the web neat and tidy.

TRAPDOOR SPIDER

This sneaky spider lives in a burrow. The entrance to its underground lair is a perfectly camouflaged, silk-hinged door. All day, the spider sits in its burrow… and waits.

Spreading out from the door are silken trip wires. If an unsuspecting insect stumbles over a wire, it alerts the spider, which darts from the trapdoor to seize its prey.

TRAPDOOR SPIDER FACTS

SIZE: body 2.5 cm (1 inch) long
HOME Americas, Europe, Asia
EATS: insects (e.g. crickets, grasshoppers, beetles), other spiders, small lizards

Like most spiders, the trapdoor spider uses its fangs to inject victims with a dose of venom. This paralyzes the prey so it cannot move.

Next the spider injects the body with digestive juices so the insides turn to mush. The spider's guts are too narrow to cope with solids.

WEIRD OR WHAT?

Trapdoor spiders are among the longest-lived spiders. Captive ones can outlive pet dogs or even cats. They have been known to live beyond the age of 20!

123

Crab Spider

CRAB SPIDER FACTS

SIZE: body up to 1 cm (½ inch)
HOME: worldwide in gardens and woodlands
EATS: flies and bees

Crab spiders are masters of disguise. Their clever camouflage allows them to launch surprise attacks and ambush their prey.

This spider's pink body makes it hard to spot against the petals of a flower. It's waiting to catch a visiting insect.

This crab spider has the perfect disguise. Its splashy markings and lumpy body make it look just like fresh bird poo. No wonder it's called the bird dung crab spider!

WEIRD OR WHAT?

Some crab spider species are like chameleons. They can change colour to match the flower they are on!

Gotcha! This crab spider has ambushed a bee.

WHIP SPIDER

Whip spiders are not true spiders, but they are arachnids.

They are named for their long front legs, which are used as sense organs. By waving these 'whips' around, the whip spider can locate prey.

WEIRD OR WHAT?

Young whip spiders use their whips another way - to stay in touch. They stretch them out to stroke their mum, brothers and sisters!

WHIP SPIDER FACTS

SIZE: body 4 cm (1½ inches) long
HOME: worldwide in tropical and subtropical regions
EATS: insects, small lizards, frogs

Like their namesakes, wolf spiders are good hunters with excellent eyesight. They don't go out in packs, though. As adults they live and hunt alone.

WOLF SPIDER FACTS

SIZE: body 1 mm–3 cm (0.04–1 inch) long (there are 2,300 species)
HOME: worldwide
EATS: insects, small arachnids

WOLF SPIDER

WEIRD OR WHAT?

A wolf spider mum frees her newly-hatched spiderlings from their egg sac by tearing it open with her fangs.

Wolf spiders are the most caring spider mums. The female carries her eggs around in a bag at the end of her body, next to her spinnerets.

CREDITS

Photo acknowledgements:

Alamy: pp 48c (Steve Smith), 51t (Steve Smith); Corbis: cover, pp 5 (Norbert Wu/Science Faction), 6b (Ralph A Clevenger), 13 (Ralph A Clevenger), 19 (Richard Herrmann/Visuals Unlimited), 25 (Specialist Stock), 26t (David Wrobel/ Visuals Unlimited), 26b (Norbert Wu/ Science Faction), 27 (Visuals Unlimited), 37 (Paul A Souders), 51b (David A Northcott), 68tl (E&P Bauer), 71 (Wayne Lynch/All Canada Photos), 76b (Patricia Fogden), 77r (Nigel Pavitt), 83 (Frans Lanting), 86 (E&P Bauer), 91 (Visuals Unlimited), 93t (Volkmar Brockhaus), 98 (Roy Morsch), 101t (Frans Lanting), 102t (Visuals Unlimited), 103t (Darrell Gulin/Science Faction), 119 (Carol Hughes/Gallo Images); FLPA: pp 4 (Thomas Marent/Minden Pictures), 6tr (Birgitte Wilms/Minden Pictures), 9 (Birgitte Wilms/Minden Pictures), 11b (Birgitte Wilms/ Minden Pictures), 22 (ImageBroker), 23t (Ingo Arndt/ Minden Pictures), 23b (Gerard Lacz), 28t (Thomas Marent/Minden Pictures), 34 (Michael & Patricia Fogden/Minden Pictures), 40b (Edward Myles), 41 (Michael & Patricia Fogden/Minden Pictures), 42t (Thomas Marent/ Minden Pictures), 43b (Thomas Marent/Minden Pictures), 48t (Michael Durham/Minden Pictures), 49 (Mark Moffett/Minden Pictures), 53t (Mark Moffett/Minden Pictures), 53b (Rolf Nussbaumer/Imagebroker), 55t (Mark Moffett/Minden Pictures), 57t (Derek Middleton), 61t (Thomas Marent/Minden Pictures), 61c (Michael & Patricia Fogden/Minden Pictures), 65l (Piotr Naskrecki/Minden Pictures), 67 (Michael Durham/Minden Pictures), 70 (Sunset), 73tr (Thomas Marent), 76t (Konrad Wothe/Minden Pictures), 84t (ZSSD/Minden Pictures), 90 (Rolf Nussbaumer/Imagebroker), 94t (Malcolm Schuyl), 94b (Ingo Arndt/Minden Pictures), 104b (Fabio Pupin), 105 (Fabio Pupin), 112 (Hugh Lansdown), 123 (Mitsuhiko Imamori/Minden Pictures); Getty Images: pp 116 (David Maitland), 120 (Heidi & Hans-Jurgen Koch/Minden Pictures); iStockphoto: pp 3tl (Atelopus), 3br (Antagain), 11t (johnandersonphoto), 15 (cvdiver168), 18t (Rich Carey), 28b (PaulTessier), 29 (drop-off-dean), 30t (waikiki), 31t (larus_ov), 33b (iSailorr), 36b (JJJMaree), 38t (AYImages), 39t (miralex), 39b (cotesebastien), 40t (PaulTessier), 43t (doucettej), 44b (drop-off-dean), 46t (benjamint444); 58b (Tokle), 59t (Antagain), 60b (DanielaAgius), 79 (MindStorm-inc), 80bl (johan63), 81br (kkaplin), 82b (Bierchen), 88b (U-photo), 89 (Atelopus), 92 (U-photo), 101bl (Atelopus), 127t (Paul Tessier); Dr Jeremy Miller: p 108; NHPA: pp 32t (Stephen Dalton), 36t (Anthony Bannister), 45t (John Cancalosi), 47 (Anthony Bannister); NORFANZ Founding Parties: p 8 (Kerryn Parkinson); Oxford Scientific Films: pp 20 (Paulo De Oliveira), 69 (Richard Kirby/Timeframe Productions Ltd), 75r (Richard Kirby/Timeframe Productions Ltd), 110 (Densey Clyne); Photolibrary: p 42b (Paul Freed); 50 (Peter Arnold Images), 64 (Satoshi Kuribayashi/Oxford Scientific Films), 88t (Oxford Scientific), 95 (Paul Beard), 103b (Satyendra Tiwari/Oxford Scientific), 104t (Oxford Scientific); Photoshot: pp 3bl (David Maitland), 14b (Zafer Kizilkaya), 24 (Stephen Dalton), 74 (Andrea Ferrari), 75l (Bruce Beehler), 82t (John Cancalosi), 87t (ANT), 106tr (Photo Researchers), 109b (Stephen Dalton), 111 (James Carmichael Jr), 115t (Daniel Heuclin), 115b (Photo Researchers), 117 (David Maitland), 121 (James Carmichael Jr), 122 (Photo Researchers), 125t (Nick Garbutt); Science Photo Library: p 21 (Christian Darkin); Shutterstock: pp 3tr (bierchen), 6tl (Rich Carey), 7 (Nikita Tiunov), 10 (bierchen), 12 (bernd.neeser), 14t (Teguh Tirtaputra), 16t (Nikita Tiunov), 16b (Rich Carey), 17t (Rich Carey), 17b (stephan kerkhofs), 18b (Rich Carey), 28c (Sebastian Duda), 30b (Sebastian Duda), 31b (Eduard Kyslynskyy), 32b (Eduardo Rivero), 33t (Peter Wollinga), 35l (BMCL), 35r (kkaplin), 38b (kkaplin), 44t (Eric Isselée), 45b (fivespots), 46b (Ashley Whitworth), 48b (Liew Weng Keong), 52t (CLChang), 52b (orionmystery@flickr), 54 (orionmystery@flickr), 55b (Yenyu Shih), 56 (Johan Swanepoel), 57t (Florian Andronache), 58t (Zheltyshev), 59b (Eric Isselée), 60t (D&K Kucharscy), 61b (Liew Weng Keong), 62 (Cathy Keifer), 63 (Ultrashock), 65r (Roland Syba), 66t (Dirk Ercken), 66b (Dirk Ercken), 68tr (hironai), 68b (Charidy B), 72r (szefei), 72b (szefei), 73bl (worldswildlifewonders), 77l (hironai), 78l (ClimberJAK), 78br (Leksele), 80tl (Four Oaks), 80r (Four Oaks), 81t (Wong Hock weng), 84b (Mihai Dancaescu), 85t (Charidy B), 85b (Braam Collins), 87b (Johan Larson), 88c (Cathy Keifer), 93b (vblinov), 96 (WitR), 97tr (Cathy Keifer), 97bl (Cathy Keifer), 99t (Alex James Bramwell), 99b (Ziga Camernik), 100t (Mircea Bezergheanu), 100b (Mircea Bezergheanu), 102b (Cathy Keifer), 106tl (Emran Mohd Tamil), 106b (D&K Kucharscy), 107 (Basel101658), 109t (ex0rzist), 113 (Emran Mohd Tamil), 114 (Audrey Snider-Bell), 118 (Basel101658), 124t (D&K Kucharscy), 124b (Christian Musat), 125b (Evgeniy Ayupov), 126t (Ivan Kuzmin), 126b (Judy Whitton), 127b (orionmystery@flickr).